Science@School | Book 6A

Adapting and surviving

KU-453-083

A brief history

TODAY... 1962 In America, Rachel Carson writes a book called Silent Spring. It makes people aware of the poisonous effect that some chemicals can have on wildlife... 1865 Haekel, in Germany, uses the word ecology to talk about the way living things live in the world around them (their environment)... 1859 Charles Darwin, in Britain, writes his book (on the origin of species). It changes the way people think about evolution... 1858 Charles Darwin and Alfred Wallace, both in Britain, separately describe evolution by natural selection... 1857 Gregor Mendel, a monk in Austria, works with peas and discovers the laws of heredity...1789 Gilbert White, in Britain, writes the first book on plants and their environment... 1735 Carolus Linnaeus, in Sweden, introduces the classification of living things that is still used today. It is based on the earlier work of John Ray... 1686 John Ray, in Britain, uses the term species for a group of plants that can breed with one another... 1667 John Ray, in Britain, introduces a new classification system for plants based on the number of seeds and leaves they have... 350BC Aristotle, in Greece, classifies plants and animals. He becomes known as the father of biology... 520BC Anaximander, in Turkey, writes the first ideas of evolution...

For more information visit www.science-at-school.com

Dr Brian Knapp

Word list

These are some science words that you should look out for as you go through the book. They are shown using CAPITAL letters.

ABSORB
To soak up.

ADAPT/ADAPTATION
The way in which an animal or plant is suited to where it lives. If something is well adapted to where it lives, it will be more likely to survive.

ALGA (plural ALGAE)
A microscopic plant that cannot be seen with the naked eye. Algae float in water. When they occur in huge numbers, they give the water a green colour.

ANNUAL
A plant which grows up from a seed, flowers, produces new seeds and then dies – all in one year. In this way, annuals can quickly cover newly exposed soil. The poppy is a successful annual.

CAMOUFLAGE
The pattern of colours and the shape of some animals that allow them to blend in with their surroundings. For example, some moths are coloured and shaped like dead leaves or bark.

CANOPY
The high branches of a forest that form a thick layer of leaves. Many insects live in the canopy and never come down to the ground.

DECOMPOSERS
Animals that eat dead material such as dead leaves or dead animals. Scavenging animals, such as magpies, will eat rotting meat. Rotting meat is called carrion. This is a vital role in making sure that the environment stays clean and that the nourishment in dead material is recycled.

GERMINATE
When a seed begins to sprout, sending out its first shoot.

HABITAT
The place where a plant or animal lives.

HIBERNATE
To go into a state of very little activity. Hibernating animals sleep for much of the time they are hibernating, but some also wake up and feed from time to time. Hibernation is an adaptation to allow animals to get through a part of the year when there is little food.

LARVA (plural LARVAE)
The young stage of an insect, between an egg and a pupa. A caterpillar is the larva of a moth or butterfly.

MAMMAL
An animal that provides milk for its young.

MIGRATE
To move a long distance in search of food, warmth or a place to breed. Many birds migrate thousands of kilometres, flying between their summer and winter homes.

NOCTURNAL
An animal that is most active at night.

PERENNIAL
A plant that grows a bit more each year and has a lifespan of several years. Trees are the longest-living perennial plants, sometimes living for thousands of years.

PUPA (plural PUPAE)
The inactive stage between a larva and an adult insect. Many insects survive the winter as a pupa or as eggs.

RODENT
A gnawing animal that has very large, chisel-shaped front teeth. Their teeth are always growing and so are never worn completely away. Rats, mice and squirrels are all rodents.

TAP ROOT
A long central root of some plants that goes deep into the ground in search of water.

TERRITORY
The region that an animal uses to find its food and to mate. Animals defend their territory in different ways.

Weblink: www.science-at-school.com

DUDLEY PUBLIC LIBRARIES

The loan of this book may be renewed if not required by other readers, by contacting the Library from which it was borrowed.

CP/494

Schools Library and Information Service

S00000151954

Contents

POOLE PUBLIC LIBRARIES

L 45764

151954   SQ

J514.5

Weblink: www.science-at-school.com

A place called home

Every living thing has to find a place where it can live, find food and protect itself from others. Here is what happens in an oak tree.

Just like us, animals and plants have a place where they live – a kind of home. It may be in a river bank, a hillside or in the branches of an oak tree. It is a place where the animal or plant finds food, shelter and some protection from its enemies. We call this natural home a **HABITAT**.

Living with others

When you look around at the homes of animals and plants, you find that each living thing lives where it is best **ADAPTED** to survive. You will see this in many of the pages of this book. You will also find that many living things depend in some way on one another, making up a great living family (community).

An oak tree (Picture 1) is not only suited to where it lives, but it is also home to many other plants and animals who depend on the tree for food and shelter.

The oak tree

A fully-grown oak tree may be 30 to 35 metres tall and spread its branches nearly as wide. Its many leaves allow it to soak up the light that it needs to make its own food and it gets water and other nourishment from the ground. The oak tree survives where it does because it is adapted to cope with a cold winter. It does this first by shedding its leaves in autumn, and then by not growing during the winter.

Many lodgers

The oak tree provides a home for more kinds of animal than any other woodland tree. Scientists have counted 30 different kinds of birds that make their home in oak trees.

They are not alone. Many insects also use the oak as a home – oaks contain over 200 different kinds of moth alone!

How does the tree cope with all these hungry lodgers eating its leaves and fruits (acorns)? A single oak tree produces up to a hundred thousand acorns a year! With so many, some are bound not to get eaten. Each oak needs only one of the acorns it has produced to grow into a tree each century for the woodland to survive.

▶ (Picture 1) An oak tree provides many places that can be used as homes. Beetles live in the roots, in the cracks of the bark and some even burrow under the bark and into the wood. Caterpillars munch away at the soft leaves.

The angles of the branches make roosting and nesting sites for birds. Natural hollows provide homes for squirrels, owls and even bats.

Summary
- Plants and animals survive in a place because they are adapted to live in it.
- Each habitat contains many different kinds of living things.

Weblink: www.science-at-school.com

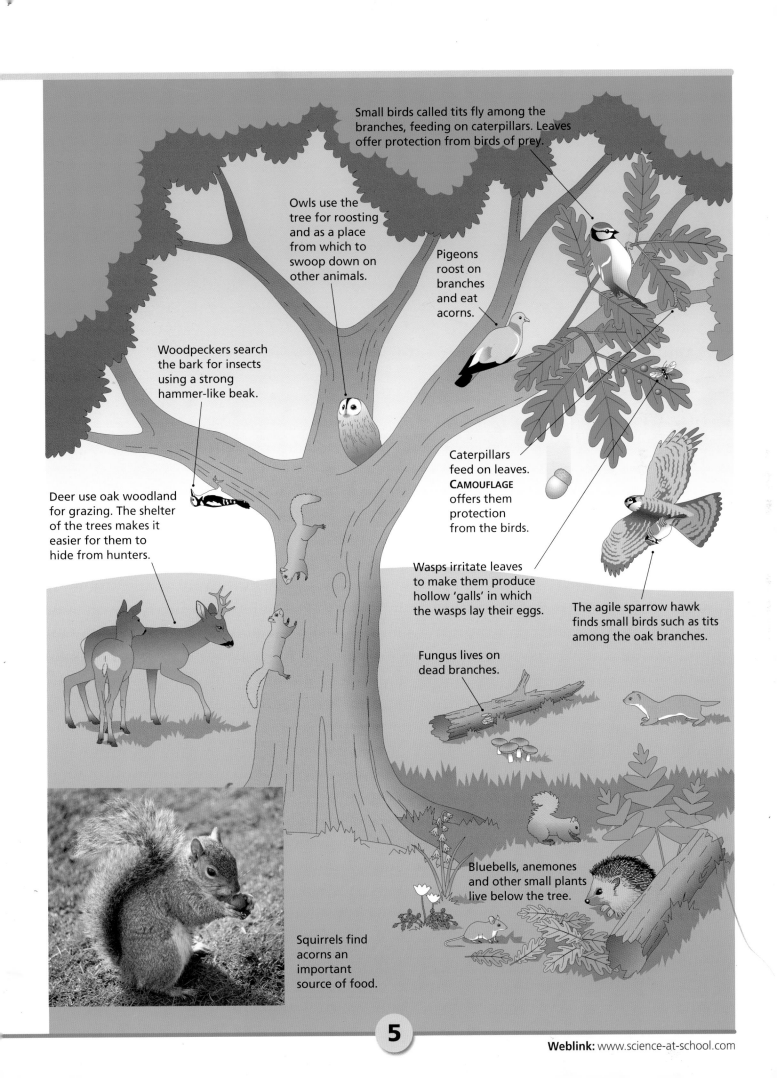

Small birds called tits fly among the branches, feeding on caterpillars. Leaves offer protection from birds of prey.

Owls use the tree for roosting and as a place from which to swoop down on other animals.

Pigeons roost on branches and eat acorns.

Woodpeckers search the bark for insects using a strong hammer-like beak.

Caterpillars feed on leaves. CAMOUFLAGE offers them protection from the birds.

Deer use oak woodland for grazing. The shelter of the trees makes it easier for them to hide from hunters.

Wasps irritate leaves to make them produce hollow 'galls' in which the wasps lay their eggs.

The agile sparrow hawk finds small birds such as tits among the oak branches.

Fungus lives on dead branches.

Bluebells, anemones and other small plants live below the tree.

Squirrels find acorns an important source of food.

Weblink: www.science-at-school.com

How plants defend themselves

If living things are to survive, they must have lots of ways of protecting themselves.

Plants are food for animals. This means that plants are always being eaten (Picture 1). Sometimes plants are also affected by fire or damaged by storms or drought. But the world is still full of plants. So how do they survive?

▲ (Picture 3) Stinging nettles protect themselves with poisons held in tiny hollow spines.

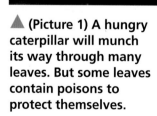

▲ (Picture 1) A hungry caterpillar will munch its way through many leaves. But some leaves contain poisons to protect themselves.

▲ (Picture 2) A rose plant defends itself with the thorns on its branches. It also grows new shoots very quickly if old branches are damaged.

Weblink: www.science-at-school.com

How plants protect themselves

Plants have many ways of protecting themselves from attack. Some plants have poisons in their leaves so that hungry animals will avoid them. Others surround themselves with sharp spines or thorns (Picture 2). Still others have poisons held in tiny needles (Picture 3).

If all this fails, and the leaves still get eaten or the branches destroyed by wind or fire, then plants will grow new shoots from just below the damaged area.

The need to regrow is so important to a plant that you can even cut some trees down to the ground and shoots will soon appear from the stumps.

Bracken is a good example of a plant that uses all sorts of tricks to survive (Picture 4). This has made it one of the world's most successful plants.

Summary

- Plants are food for animals and so are often damaged.
- All plants need ways of regrowing.
- Some plants survive by keeping most animals away.

▼ (Picture 4) Bracken and some of its many defences.

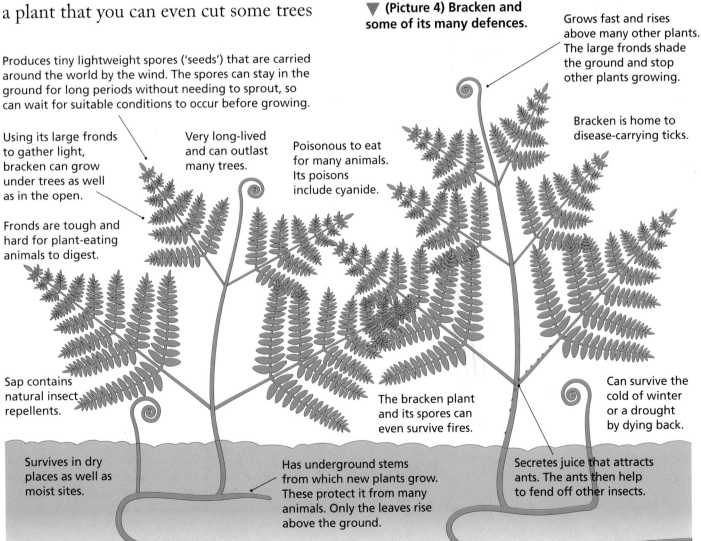

Produces tiny lightweight spores ('seeds') that are carried around the world by the wind. The spores can stay in the ground for long periods without needing to sprout, so can wait for suitable conditions to occur before growing.

Using its large fronds to gather light, bracken can grow under trees as well as in the open.

Fronds are tough and hard for plant-eating animals to digest.

Very long-lived and can outlast many trees.

Poisonous to eat for many animals. Its poisons include cyanide.

Grows fast and rises above many other plants. The large fronds shade the ground and stop other plants growing.

Bracken is home to disease-carrying ticks.

Sap contains natural insect repellents.

The bracken plant and its spores can even survive fires.

Can survive the cold of winter or a drought by dying back.

Survives in dry places as well as moist sites.

Has underground stems from which new plants grow. These protect it from many animals. Only the leaves rise above the ground.

Secretes juice that attracts ants. The ants then help to fend off other insects.

Weblink: www.science-at-school.com

Sharing the same place

Many different plants can live in the same place if they grow and flower at different times of the year.

Every kind of living thing needs water, warmth and nourishment. Plants also need light. So how do so many kinds of living things share the same place (habitat)?

In fact, many living things are able to use the same space if they use it in different ways or at different times of the year. In Picture 1 you can see how different plants use the same woodland through the year.

Growing early

Some plants even begin to grow in winter. Snowdrops are the first to shoot, sometimes even flowering while snow is still on the ground. As the months pass, they are followed by other plants.

The first plants grow from bulbs, tubers and thick underground stems. They use the food they have stored from the previous year. They do not need to wait for the ground to warm up, or the sun to shine strongly, in order to begin their annual growth.

So, by late spring the early plants have all flowered and set seeds almost before the other plants have even started putting out leaves.

Summer leaves

By late spring, the forest floor has warmed up enough for more plants to begin to shoot (Picture 2).

▼ (Picture 1) Seasonal changes on the forest floor.

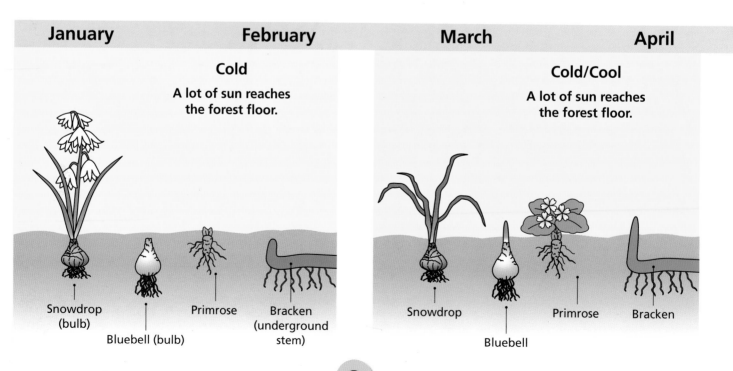

Weblink: www.science-at-school.com

(Picture 2) This picture, taken in May, shows bluebells already fading by the time the brackens develop their first fronds. Notice that the lower flowers have already turned into green seed pods. Now the leaves will wither as the plant takes back the nourishment into its bulb that it will need for next spring. The first leaves on the trees can also be seen in the background.

Summer woodland plants such as bracken do not have bulbs and so do not have a large store of nourishment. This is why it takes them more time to start growing.

But just as these new plants burst into life, trees also start putting out leaves and the ground becomes shady. Summer plants therefore have to be good at growing in the shade. That is, they have adapted to live in a partly shady place. This is why they have leaves that last for many months, so they have longer to make the food that will help the roots below the surface grow.

Summary

- Plants share the same space by growing at different times of the year.
- Plants that grow at the same time must have special ways of dealing with shady conditions.

May

June

Cool

Some sun reaches the forest floor.

Snowdrop   Primrose   Bracken

Bluebell

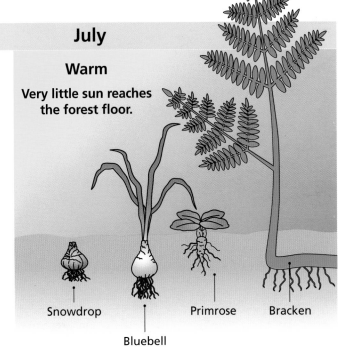

July

Warm

Very little sun reaches the forest floor.

Snowdrop   Primrose   Bracken

Bluebell

9

Weblink: www.science-at-school.com

Woodland through the seasons

A woodland changes dramatically through the seasons. The lives of both plants and animals are adapted to the changes.

You have already seen how a single oak can be a home for many animals. When oaks grow together they make an oak woodland. Here you can see, all in one place, many of the ways of adapting described on the previous pages (Picture 1).

The canopy

Oaks grow until their branches fit together to make a covering of leaves called a **CANOPY**. This is how the leaves get the light they need from the Sun. The canopy is thick with leaves and acorns for part of the year, but in winter the leaves are gone and the branches bare, windswept and cold.

The woodland floor

Many plants and animals live below the canopy. Buds, leaves, flowers, falling fruit and nuts are all food for animals that live on the woodland floor.

Adapting to the seasons

Because the food supply of the woodland changes so much with the seasons, the way the animals behave also changes.

▼ (Picture 1) An oak woodland through the four seasons.

Winter

Birds adapted to the cold feed on seeds, berries and shoots in the undergrowth.

Holly bush produces berries.

Insects survive as eggs. Many stay in the soil or sheltered under leaves or bark until spring.

Snowdrop

Squirrels use the nuts they stored in autumn.

Hedgehog hibernates in bracken.

Spring

First leaves start to sprout on trees.

Birds attracted to insects on tree.

Caterpillars hatch from eggs.

Birds that are not adapted to the cold winter return from winter homes in warmer parts of the world.

Primrose flowering is almost over.

Bluebells begin to flower.

Weblink: www.science-at-school.com

Many insects spend the winter as eggs or **PUPAE** (Picture 2) because they have no leaves to eat. Hedgehogs can eat worms, slugs, spiders and insects. But as their food supply dwindles, hedgehogs **HIBERNATE** and sleep during most of the winter season.

Wood mice do not hibernate. They eat seeds and bark in the winter and buds and seedlings in spring when the plants begin to shoot. They also eat insects during the summer and blackberries and mushrooms in autumn. Squirrels survive the winter on the acorns and other seeds they buried in the ground during the autumn.

The woodland has far fewer birds in winter because many **MIGRATE** (fly away) to warmer lands. Blue tits and other birds that stay for the winter are adapted to survive the cold and the scarce food supplies.

▶ (Picture 2) This superbly camouflaged butterfly chrysalis (a kind of pupa) is about two centimetres long. It hangs in the shelter of a twig, branch or leaf. In the winter, many adult moths and butterflies die, but their offspring spend the winter as an egg or as a pupa, often underground.

Summary

- **The woodland floor changes dramatically through the year.**
- **In winter, when there is little food, most animals are not active.**
- **Many birds fly away to warmer places during the winter.**

Summer

The canopy is a plentiful source of food for insects. Birds eat insects.

Trees spread their leaves to get as much sunlight as possible.

Undergrowth fully grown.

Squirrels eat fruits and nuts.

Hedgehog is active, eating insects and earthworms.

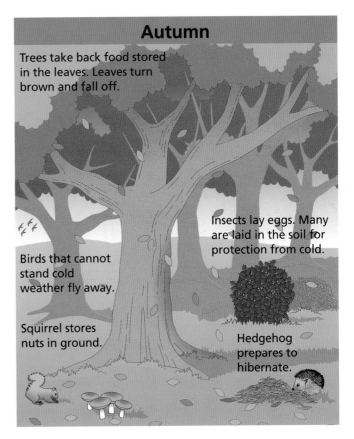

Autumn

Trees take back food stored in the leaves. Leaves turn brown and fall off.

Insects lay eggs. Many are laid in the soil for protection from cold.

Birds that cannot stand cold weather fly away.

Squirrel stores nuts in ground.

Hedgehog prepares to hibernate.

11

Ponds

Ponds contain still water. The water is shallow at the edge and deeper in the middle, giving lots of opportunities for different kinds of life.

Ponds are less affected than the land by changes in the weather. Temperatures do not rise so high in the day, nor fall so far at night. In winter, only the surface of the pond freezes over.

This means that pond life does not have to adapt so much to the weather in order to survive (Picture 1).

▼ **(Picture 1) The pond environment.**

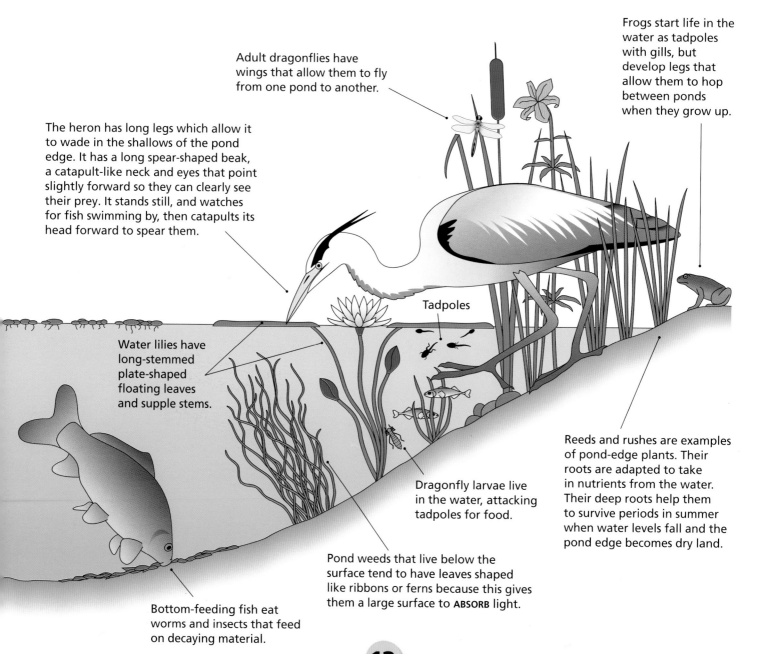

Adult dragonflies have wings that allow them to fly from one pond to another.

Frogs start life in the water as tadpoles with gills, but develop legs that allow them to hop between ponds when they grow up.

The heron has long legs which allow it to wade in the shallows of the pond edge. It has a long spear-shaped beak, a catapult-like neck and eyes that point slightly forward so they can clearly see their prey. It stands still, and watches for fish swimming by, then catapults its head forward to spear them.

Tadpoles

Water lilies have long-stemmed plate-shaped floating leaves and supple stems.

Reeds and rushes are examples of pond-edge plants. Their roots are adapted to take in nutrients from the water. Their deep roots help them to survive periods in summer when water levels fall and the pond edge becomes dry land.

Dragonfly larvae live in the water, attacking tadpoles for food.

Pond weeds that live below the surface tend to have leaves shaped like ribbons or ferns because this gives them a large surface to ABSORB light.

Bottom-feeding fish eat worms and insects that feed on decaying material.

12

Plants in a pond

Ponds do not have many large plants in them. But they still contain food for animals. You may be surprised to know that the pond is full of plants you cannot see. This is because most of the plants are tiny and usually only visible with a microscope. They are called **ALGAE** (Picture 2).

The larger plants are mostly rooted in the pond mud. The plants that live around the edge of the pond have only their roots in water, and their stems and leaves in the air.

Farther from the edge are the plants that have leaves floating on the surface, but stems and roots in the water. The stems do not need to be stiff, because they are supported by the water.

Finally, there are plants that live totally beneath the surface but still have roots in the pond bottom. These are the pond weeds. They still need light, so they must stay close to the surface, but they get everything else they need from the water.

Animals in a pond

Most of the food in a pond is tiny algae. Lots of small animals, such as water fleas, eat the algae.

These plant-eating animals are, in turn, prey to bigger pond animals, such as insects, fish, frogs and birds. The smaller animals survive by breeding in huge numbers.

All the waste and dead matter produced by plants and animals settles to the bottom of the pond, where it is used as food for yet more animals. These include many insect **LARVAE** and some worms and water lice.

All pond animals have to be adapted to moving between ponds to find more space. There are many ways they do this. Frogs, for example, change from water-living tadpoles to air-breathing frogs. By contrast, the eggs of fish stick to the feet of birds that fly between ponds.

▼ **(Picture 2) Pond water seen through a microscope.**

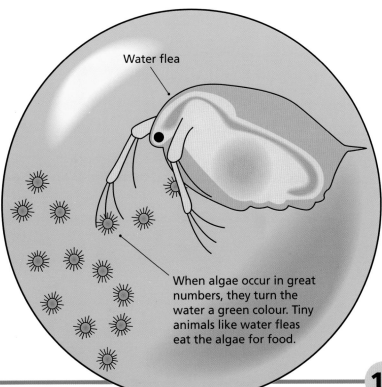

Water flea

When algae occur in great numbers, they turn the water a green colour. Tiny animals like water fleas eat the algae for food.

Summary
- **Plants change in shape depending on the depth of water they live in.**
- **Many animals rely on eating algae or dead matter on the pond floor.**
- **All living things must have ways of moving their offspring between ponds.**

13

Rivers

Rivers often begin as fast-flowing streams with rocky beds, then get slower and flow over muddy beds as they near the sea. As a result, rivers contain many different types of life.

Rivers flow from high land, where they have stony beds, to lowlands, where their beds are made of mud and silt, to the sea where rivers become tidal and where sandbanks and mudflats are common (Picture 1). Quite different types of plants and animals are adapted to live in each part of the river's course.

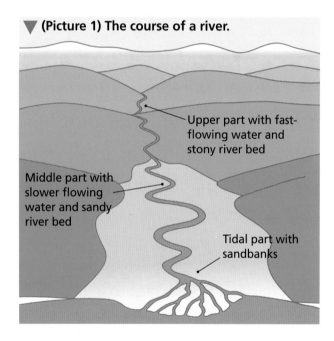

▼ (Picture 1) The course of a river.

Upper part with fast-flowing water and stony river bed

Middle part with slower flowing water and sandy river bed

Tidal part with sandbanks

The upper part of a river

Rivers flowing quickly over stony beds would sweep many plants and animals away, so most river animals found here are strong swimmers, or can shelter between the rocks (Picture 2). Here, animals feed on leaves falling into the water, or catch insects on or in the water.

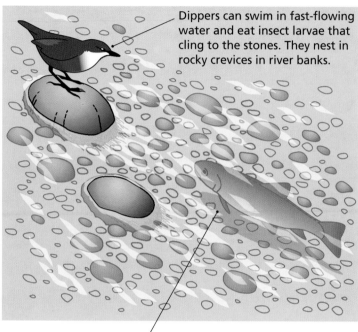

Dippers can swim in fast-flowing water and eat insect larvae that cling to the stones. They nest in rocky crevices in river banks.

Fish such as trout swim strongly but, even so, they prefer the pools, while most smaller creatures have to live in the shelter of rocks.

▲ (Picture 2) The upper reaches of a river, where the bed is stony.

The middle part of a river

Downstream, the water flows slowly enough for sand, silt and mud to settle out (Picture 3). Many animals have made use of this soft material to protect themselves. Animals such as mussels dig deep burrows. Rooted plants can also grow here.

Most small animals feed on dead leaves that sink to the river bottom. More varieties of fish are found here, including those that are less strong swimmers. River banks are soft and provide a home for

Weblink: www.science-at-school.com

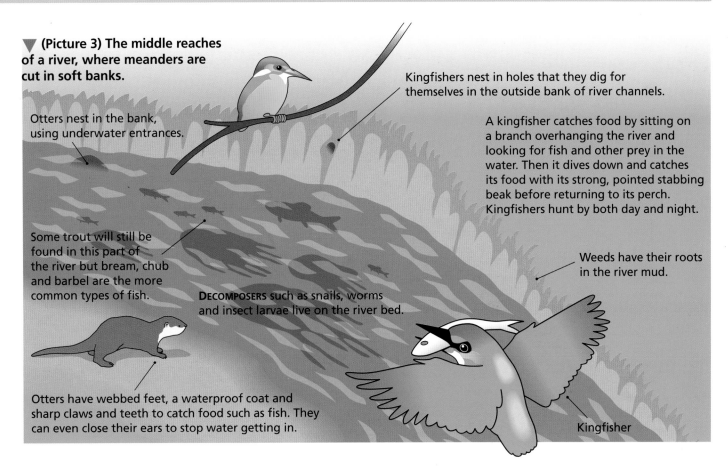

▼ (Picture 3) The middle reaches of a river, where meanders are cut in soft banks.

Otters nest in the bank, using underwater entrances.

Kingfishers nest in holes that they dig for themselves in the outside bank of river channels.

A kingfisher catches food by sitting on a branch overhanging the river and looking for fish and other prey in the water. Then it dives down and catches its food with its strong, pointed stabbing beak before returning to its perch. Kingfishers hunt by both day and night.

Some trout will still be found in this part of the river but bream, chub and barbel are the more common types of fish.

DECOMPOSERS such as snails, worms and insect larvae live on the river bed.

Weeds have their roots in the river mud.

Otters have webbed feet, a waterproof coat and sharp claws and teeth to catch food such as fish. They can even close their ears to stop water getting in.

Kingfisher

burrowing birds such as kingfishers and **MAMMALS** such as otters and water voles.

The tidal part of a river

At the mouth of the river the water is very sluggish and the bottom muds become thick. More plants can take root and huge numbers of burrowing animals, such as worms and snails, can thrive. Wading birds of all kinds are adapted to find the food buried in the sand and mud (Picture 4).

Summary

- **Habitats change as the river changes along its course.**
- **So that they can live together, different wading birds have different shaped beaks to find different food.**

▼ (Picture 4) The tidal reaches of the river, where mudflats and sandbanks are common.

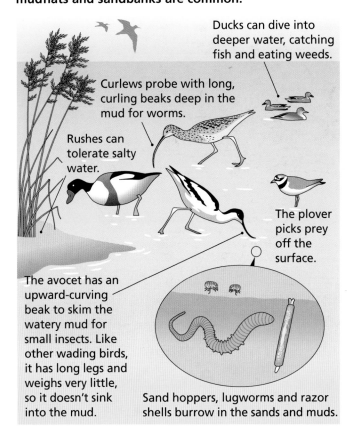

Ducks can dive into deeper water, catching fish and eating weeds.

Curlews probe with long, curling beaks deep in the mud for worms.

Rushes can tolerate salty water.

The plover picks prey off the surface.

The avocet has an upward-curving beak to skim the watery mud for small insects. Like other wading birds, it has long legs and weighs very little, so it doesn't sink into the mud.

Sand hoppers, lugworms and razor shells burrow in the sands and muds.

15

Weblink: www.science-at-school.com

Meadows

A meadow is a place where grasses and flowering plants grow and where there are no trees. They mainly exist because of the way people farm the land.

Meadows are places where grasses and other flowering plants thrive, but where trees are rare (Picture 1). Natural meadows are only common on high mountains where trees cannot grow. But they are also found in valley bottoms where farmers have cut down the trees to make grazing land for animals (Picture 2).

Many varieties of plants

As animals graze, they eat the shoots of trees so new trees can't grow.

▼ **(Picture 1) This meadow consists of a variety of grasses whose flowers are on the top of tall thin stems. Many other plants can also be seen, including the yellow flower of a buttercup.**

Meadows have more variety of grasses and flowering plants than any other place. Over 500 kinds of plants have been found in one meadow. This is because trees do not shade them out.

A wealth of animals

Even though farmers want the meadow to be used for their animals, there is also much wildlife. This is because meadows are a much better place to find food than woodlands.

Many birds nest in among the plants. The skylark is a common meadow bird that eats seeds and insects. It makes its nest on the ground and camouflages it.

Weblink: www.science-at-school.com

Many hunters

With many animals using the meadow for food, meadows attract many winged hunters such as hawks, that patrol by day, or owls, that patrol by night.

Burrowing is one way to make a home that is safe from these hunters. Rabbits and voles are among many burrowing animals that can thrive in a meadow.

Below the surface

The plants on the surface shed lots of leaves that rot and become food for soil animals. The dung of grazing animals can be another source of food. Below the soil there may be tons of earthworms in each hectare of meadow. And there will be a small army of moles and other tunnelling animals trying to eat them. Tunnelling animals like moles have bodies shaped so they can push themselves through the soil. They have strong, short, front legs and spade-like paws with sharp claws so that they can dig rapidly.

Summary
- Meadows are places of great variety.
- With so much food, meadows are home to many animals.

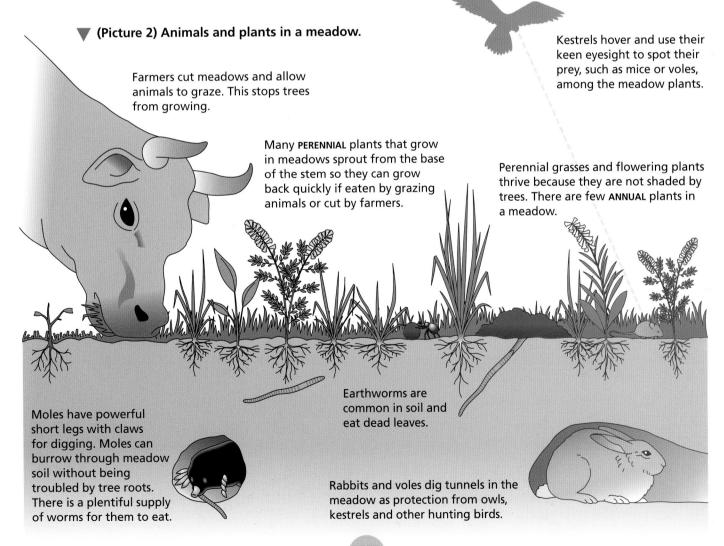

▼ **(Picture 2) Animals and plants in a meadow.**

Farmers cut meadows and allow animals to graze. This stops trees from growing.

Many PERENNIAL plants that grow in meadows sprout from the base of the stem so they can grow back quickly if eaten by grazing animals or cut by farmers.

Kestrels hover and use their keen eyesight to spot their prey, such as mice or voles, among the meadow plants.

Perennial grasses and flowering plants thrive because they are not shaded by trees. There are few ANNUAL plants in a meadow.

Moles have powerful short legs with claws for digging. Moles can burrow through meadow soil without being troubled by tree roots. There is a plentiful supply of worms for them to eat.

Earthworms are common in soil and eat dead leaves.

Rabbits and voles dig tunnels in the meadow as protection from owls, kestrels and other hunting birds.

Weblink: www.science-at-school.com

Rock pools

Some animals can live in rock pools, even though they are battered by waves, if they are adapted in the right way.

Rock pools are bowl-shaped hollows which hold sea-water when the tide goes out (Picture 1).

A rock pool is a very difficult place to live in because conditions are continually changing. For example, rock pools can get very hot on a sunny day, and cold at night. When the tide is out, some animals close up so they don't dry out.

▼ **(Picture 1) The rock pool environment.**

Waves and tides

Twice a day – as the tide comes in and as it goes out – plants and animals must be able to stand up to the battering of breaking waves by holding fast to rocks or sheltering in some way. Clearly, a rock

The oystercatcher has a chisel-shaped bill to open limpets and other shells or to prise them off rocks.

Limpets have streamlined shells so they are not easily pulled off the rock by breaking waves. Their shells are thick, so they do not crack easily if they are hit by pebbles in the waves.

The sea anemone closes up tight during low tide. It only opens when the sea rises – then it sends out stinging tentacles.

The flexible, waving fronds of seaweeds move with the waves and so are not broken by them. Unlike land plants, they take in all of their nourishment from the sea-water through their fronds instead of their roots.

Starfish can use their feet to hang on to the rocky surface of the pool while waves are breaking.

Tiny algae that float in the sea-water are the food for many animals, such as limpets and mussels.

A blenny is a typical small rock pool fish. It has eyes on top of its head so that it can spot a bird trying to stab it from above. Its mottled colours help to camouflage it among the pebbles at the bottom of the rock pool.

Hermit crabs use empty shells to protect their soft bodies. They eat food that gets washed in by waves.

Weblink: www.science-at-school.com

pool is no place for large living things or those that are in any way delicate.

Animals like crabs, shrimps and small fish take shelter from waves under rocky ledges or stones. Some can burrow into the sandy bottom of the pool.

Finding food

Rock pools do not contain much food, so animals must be able to survive by eating only when the tide comes in. With nothing to eat, many animals, such as sea anemones and limpets, close up tight and wait for a new supply of food to arrive with the next tide (Picture 2).

▲ (Picture 2) Rock pools at low tide, with waves breaking in the distance. Notice the sandy bed of the pool, and the seaweed. Colonies of mussels are clinging to the bare rock above the pool. These are shown in more detail by the picture on the right. See how they live together for added protection from the waves.

Depending on one another

Each of the creatures in a shallow, seaweed-free rock pool is easy prey for hunters such as birds. This is why larger pools, with lots of seaweed to hide under, are home to more small animals than open pools.

The seaweed has extra benefits. It puts oxygen into the water and so helps more water-life to survive the period between tides. At the same time, the pool animals release wastes that contain the nourishment the seaweed needs. In this way, many of the living things in a rock pool depend on one another.

Offspring

How do living things produce young in such a battering environment? Many send out huge numbers of eggs which hatch in the open sea. Only when the young are nearly fully grown do they seek a pool to live in. Others shelter their young until they are grown up enough to fend for themselves.

Summary

- Only a small number of living things can survive the battering of a rock pool.
- When the tide is out, many animals close up so that they don't dry out.
- Many living things in rock pools have special ways of protecting themselves from the waves.

Weblink: www.science-at-school.com

Mountains

Mountains are places with cool summers and harsh, snowy winters. They are places where only the specially adapted can survive.

High mountains experience long, cold, snowy winters and short, wet, cloudy summers. Not only is the weather harsh, but soils are thin and stony and have little nourishment in them.

Mountain plants

Few plants can survive such conditions. Some of those that are adapted to cope with the cold and wind are called alpines. Most alpines are perennials. Few annual plants grow on mountains – it takes many years of slow, determined growth for a plant just to get big enough to flower (Picture 1). Alpines are small, woody perennial plants that hug the ground, or shelter between boulders, growing just a little each year in the brief summer.

Mountain animals

Because mountain plants are scarce and grow slowly, there is not much food for animals on a mountain. Each animal needs a large **TERRITORY** in which to search for food (Picture 2). A single golden eagle, for example, needs a territory of 200 square kilometres!

▼ **(Picture 1) How alpine plants are adapted to the harsh mountain environment.**

Alpines need to store as much heat as possible. Many are tufted, have furry leaves, and grow in dense, low bushes. Many even make their own antifreeze. The leaves are dark green, to soak up as much of the Sun's heat as possible.

Hardy grasses

Sedges and mosses grow where water has been trapped and create bogs.

Insulating snow cover protects plants in winter.

Lichens cling to rocks.

Heather

Edelweiss

Thin, poor soils

All alpine plants need to be adapted for dry conditions. This may seem strange when they may be covered in snow for half the year. But the water in snow is locked up as ice and so plants cannot use it. Then, as soon as the snow melts, harsh winds dry out the ground. To cope with this, even plants that seem tiny when seen on the surface may have deep **TAP ROOTS** that seek water far underground.

Alpines have to make good use of the short growing season. As soon as the snow melts, they shoot, flower and set seed – giving the spectacular blossoms for which mountains are so famous. The entire growing season may be only three months.

Weblink: www.science-at-school.com

(Picture 2) Some of the many adaptations that animals have to help them survive in the mountains.

Golden eagle

Great height allows birds of prey to survey a large area – important when prey is scarce.

Cliff caves provide safe nesting sites and 'launch pads' for mountain birds of prey such as eagles and ravens.

In winter ptarmigan do not hibernate. They scratch down through the snow to browse on shrubs and lichens. They burrow under the snow to protect themselves from the weather whilst they sleep.

Mountain goats are skilled climbers and can climb on near-vertical cliffs to reach patches of vegetation. However, even they must migrate to lower altitudes in winter because the high mountain areas are deeply covered in snow.

Few, if any, plants can grow on the bare rocky cliffs on mountain tops.

Red deer graze on natural meadows in summer.

Lynx

Raven

Ptarmigan

Alpine plants

Marmot

Tree line. The upper limit where a forest can grow.

Few butterfly species are adapted to high altitudes because they need warmer conditions.

It is common for animals that use camouflage to change their colour with the seasons. Ptarmigan and mountain hare both turn white in winter. In summer, their coats are brown.

The dipper is adapted to fast flowing mountain streams

Apollo butterfly

Mountain hare

Few animals remain in the mountains during winter. Most hibernate until the snow melts in spring. The small number of animals that continue to be active in the winter snow are especially hardy and change colour to white in order to stay camouflaged in the snow.

Many **RODENTS** in high mountains live in a network of tunnels in the rocky soil. These provide a place to hibernate in winter. However, as rodents such as marmots (above) and voles (below) search among the rocks for food, they are easily spotted by predators such as eagles, weasels, lynx and foxes. To escape being caught, they are camouflaged by the colour of their fur and quickly take shelter in the rocks.

Summary
- Mountain plants grow slowly and hug the ground.
- Most animals hibernate through the winter.
- Some animals change colour from summer to winter in order to remain camouflaged and avoid being eaten.

Weblink: www.science-at-school.com

Deserts

10

Deserts are mainly hot places with very little rainfall. Very few plants and animals can survive such difficult conditions.

Deserts are places where the rainfall is small and very unreliable. Most deserts are hot and sunny, so coping with drought is the main problem for any living thing in a desert (Picture 1).

Plants with a short life

Plants are adapted in two ways. One group are annuals, whose seeds lie in the desert soil until rain comes. Then, they race to **GERMINATE**, grow, flower and set seed before the ground dries out. This may all happen in just a few weeks.

Plants that grow slowly

The other group of plants are perennials. Between rainfalls they simply stop growing.

Some desert perennials have deep tap roots to find water, even when it has seeped deep underground. To prevent losing water, they have small, waxy leaves with few pores.

Others, such as the cactus, store water in fleshy stems than can swell with water. They have no leaves at all: their green stems make all the food they need.

Animals in the desert

Animals, too, face the problems of getting water, avoiding the heat and finding food. Like mountains, deserts provide little food and so few animals can live there. Those that do each need a large territory if they are to find enough to eat.

Many desert animals burrow into the sand, or shelter in the shade, during the heat of the day and only come out after dark. At night, the temperature falls sharply and dew is quite common. Many animals get all the moisture they need from the late night dew.

Camels are one of the few desert animals that move about during the day. Camels can survive when they have lost almost a third of their body water. This is more than twice as much as most animals can lose. When they do find water, camels can drink a fifth of their body weight in ten minutes.

The hump of the camel is where it stores fat. This fat allows it to survive, even if it cannot find food for weeks. Camels also have thick fur to protect them from the heat, and pad-like hooves to make it possible to travel across soft sand.

Weblink: www.science-at-school.com

▼ (Picture 1) Some of the many adaptations that animals and plants have to help them survive in the desert.

Scorpions use the poisonous tip of their tail to kill their prey and defend themselves. They get all of the water they need from the food they eat.

Pincers to grab prey.

The cactus stores water in its stem, has no leaves and has protective spines to stop animals from eating it.

Eagles and vultures fly at great heights to spot prey or dead animals.

Desert foxes are **NOCTURNAL** scavengers and crafty hunters. They are able to dig out the burrows of kangaroo rats and even eat scorpions. They have large ears and eyes because they only feed at night. They have a keen sense of smell to find rotting meat.

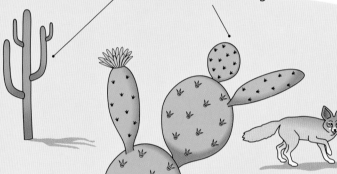

Lizards use camouflage and quick movements to escape hunters.

Sidewinder snakes move across sand in a special way, so that only a small part of their skin rests on the burning hot surface at any time. This way of moving also prevents the snakes from sinking into the soft sand.

Summary

- **Deserts are hot places with very little water and very unreliable rainfall.**
- **Plants adapt by storing water, and having long roots and small leaves.**
- **Animals have adapted by being nocturnal, or by storing water and food in their bodies.**

Kangaroo rats come out in the cool darkness of the night. Their long legs allow them to run very fast to escape predators such as snakes and foxes. They are adapted to get all the water they need from the moisture in the seeds they eat.

Plants such as the creosote bush have very long tap roots to find water. As with many plants in the desert, they also have small, leathery leaves.

23

Index

Science@School

Science@School is a series published by Atlantic Europe Publishing Company Ltd.

Atlantic Europe Publishing

Teacher's Guide
There is a Teacher's Guide to accompany this book, available only from the publisher.

CD-ROMs
There are CD-ROMs containing information to support the series. They are available from the publisher.

Dedicated Web Site
There's more information about other great Science@School packs and a wealth of supporting material available at our dedicated web site:

www.science-at-school.com

First published in 2001 by
Atlantic Europe Publishing Company Ltd

Copyright © 2001
Atlantic Europe Publishing Company Ltd

All rights reserved. No part of this publication may be reproduced, stored in a retrieval system, or transmitted in any form or by any means, electronic, mechanical, photocopying, recording or otherwise, without prior permission of the publisher.

Author
Brian Knapp, BSc, PhD

Educational Consultant
Peter Riley, BSc

Art Director
Duncan McCrae, BSc

Senior Designer
Adele Humphries, BA, PGCE

Editor
Lisa Magloff, BA

Illustrations
David Woodroffe

Designed and produced by
EARTHSCAPE EDITIONS

Reproduced in Malaysia by
Global Colour

Printed in Hong Kong by
Wing King Tong Company Ltd

Suggested cataloguing location
Knapp, Brian
    Adapting and surviving – *Science@School*
    1. Ecology – Juvenile Literature
    I. Title. II. Series
574.5

Paperback ISBN 1 86214 172 X
Hardback ISBN 1 86214 173 8

Picture credits
All photographs are from the Earthscape Editions photolibrary.

This product is manufactured from sustainable managed forests. For every tree cut down at least one more is planted.